So You Think Your Cat is a Communist

18421st Edition

INDEX

The History of Communism in Cats…………………….....1

Listen to your Cat…………………………………….……5

Signs Your Cat Went Communist!..11

Conclusion……………………………….………....……23ish

The History of Communism in Cats

In history, various things have been documented with the creation of a society of cats that were cast into the illusion of communism. War is between humans, and they tend to fight each other no matter what. But it was interesting to indulge cats in this war. While people knew that the Communist leader Lenin liked cats, and was a famous cat lover, they decided to spy on him with the help of cats. Lenin's enemies started noticing small changes in his cats and knew that his cat Господин Рукавицы (Mr. Mittens) was also looking to turn the land and it's people to a fleet of tuna boat workers. Though Mr. Mittens fell into catnip, he still pushed through many policies that some cats do to this day. *(Has a cat ever put its butthole on you face? Mr. Mittens pushed that agenda in 1923.)* He was notably not a sweetie pie smoochy smoochy.

Though the U.S. with the help of the Australian government, a grand total of 50 cats were sent to Lenin over the span of 5 years with hopes of learning everything Russia was planning during a high-tension era. Yet little did they know every cat was converted to a staunch Communist. Lenin was even known to sit at his desk while petting a cat, all the while plotting his revenge on such people he had created bitter rivalries with. He had a bout with a police officer of the time named Gadget. Lenin sat with a cat named Mad Cat and would pound on his desk repeatedly while shouting the inspector's name. However, there is no recorded record that Lenin meeting up or resolving his issues with Gadget.

Lenin died 21 January 1924 (aged 53) from asbestos poisoning from some of the first manufactured litter of the time. All 50 of his cats were given to family and friends where the kitties were free to spread their message wide.

After the market crash of the late 20's most cats were left with little choice but to turn to crime being judged by their social standpoint. Chubby Boots, a cat in the United States that kept a detailed journal at that time wrote:

The days draw ever colder as the nights feel longer. I for one am NOT going to starve as my kin. The local Butcher in town, Mr. James Kingston, has chased me off one too many times. He has been most vulgar and uses the most foul of words. "Mangy Fleabag" "Strupple Chafflemaker" He would yell as he swings a broom at me and my fellow party as we asked kindly for some delectable cow innards or a scrap of pig eye at the back door of the shop. Perhaps if we became a communist party he would surely change his stance and give us some nommy nomm.

So ironically, he followed through, and Boots fell into the Communist party and changed the course of American history forever.

The only known picture of Chubby Boots

As most cats were in desperate need of food and a purrrpose, Chubby had no problem recruiting upwards of 50 alley cats to take up the communist ways with the promise of food and treats and no less than a week later, they owned the butcher shop that tempted them so. Kingston was never heard from again as the cats took control and of course rumors amongst the townsfolk had a nagging suspicion as their meat tasted just a little funny for some time after.

After this, word spread throughout the kitty kingdom of the butcher shop takeover and the party spread across America at record pace as the cats started to take control. People were none the wiser as the cat business sector swept the nation. The had taken stores, networks, NASA, and most of the fishing industry headfirst. There seemed to be no stopping what they could do. But, as all things do, the general cat got to complacent and as they slowly lost their grip on the nation, they settled on a general spy network. More often than not, they would settle down with an unsuspecting family and only report back to the leaders of the fishing industry when they needed or saw fit. They lost control of the shops and most networks they once ruled over and settled to a quieter and more leisure setting.

Listen to your Cat

The most important thing you can do is listen. The first sign that your feline friend might be a communist could be the most obvious one. What does he or she say? Is your kitty quiet or does your cat strut around the house asking for the former Chinese Communist ruler Mao Zedong?

A classic Commie Kittie salute

I have heard it dozens of times, where somebody is totally oblivious as their little four-legged fluffball is constantly talking about Mao! That's right, at all hours of the day and night, some cats just say Mao, Mao, Mao. If this sound all too familiar, then **you are in trouble!** You, without a doubt need to learn as much as you can about the CCP ruler Mao and fast. Luckily here is a brief but detailed hissstory so you can meet your cat on the same level.

Mao was the son of a prosperous peasant in Shaoshan, Hunan. He had a Chinese nationalist and an anti-imperialist outlook early in his life and was particularly influenced by the events of the Xinhai Revolution of 1911 and May Fourth Movement of 1919. He later adopted Marxism–Leninism while working at Peking University, and became a founding member of the Chinese Communist Party (CCP), leading the Autumn Harvest Uprising in 1927. During the Chinese Civil War between the Kuomintang (KMT) and the CCP, Mao helped to create the Chinese Workers' and Peasants' Red Army, led the Jiangxi Soviet's radical land policies, and ultimately became head of the CCP during the Long March. Although the CCP temporarily allied with the KMT under the United Front during the Second Sino-Japanese War (1937–1945), China's civil war resumed after Japan's surrender and in 1949 Mao's forces defeated the Nationalist government, which withdrew to Taiwan.

On October 1, 1949, Mao proclaimed the foundation of the PRC, a Marxist–Leninist single-party state controlled by the CCP. In the following years he solidified his control through campaigns against landlords, suppression of "counter-revolutionaries", "Three-anti and Five-anti Campaigns" and through a psychological victory in the Korean War, which altogether resulted in the deaths of several million Chinese. From 1953 to 1958, Mao played an important role in enforcing planned economy in China, constructing the first

Constitution of the PRC, launching the industrialisation program, and initiating the "Two Bombs, One Satellite" project. In 1955–1957, Mao launched the Sufan movement and the Anti-Rightist Campaign, with at least 550,000 people persecuted in the latter, most of whom were intellectuals and dissidents. In 1958, he launched the Great Leap Forward that aimed to rapidly transform China's economy from agrarian to industrial, which led to the deadliest famine in history and the deaths of 15–55 million people between 1958 and 1962. In 1963, Mao launched the Socialist Education Movement, and in 1966 he initiated the Cultural Revolution, a program to remove "counter-revolutionary" elements in Chinese society which lasted 10 years and was marked by violent class struggle, widespread destruction of cultural artifacts, and an unprecedented elevation of Mao's cult of personality. Tens of millions of people were persecuted during the Revolution, while the estimated number of deaths ranges from hundreds of thousands to millions, including Liu Shaoqi, the 2nd Chairman of the PRC. After years of ill health, Mao suffered a series of heart attacks in 1976 and died at the age of 82. During Mao's era, China's population grew from around 550 million to over 900 million while the government did not strictly enforce its family planning policy. The Chinese

Communist Party was founded by Chen Duxiu and Li Dazhao in the French concession of Shanghai in 1921 as a study society and informal network. Mao set up a Changsha branch, also establishing a branch of the Socialist Youth Corps and a Cultural Book Society which opened a bookstore to propagate revolutionary literature throughout Hunan. He was involved in the movement for Hunan autonomy, in the hope that a Hunanese constitution would increase civil liberties and make his revolutionary activity easier. When the movement was successful in establishing provincial autonomy under a new warlord, Mao forgot his involvement. By 1921, small Marxist groups existed in Shanghai, Beijing, Changsha, Wuhan, Guangzhou, and Jinan; it was decided to hold a central meeting, which began in Shanghai on July 23, 1921. The first session of the National Congress of the Chinese Communist Party was attended by 13 delegates, Mao included. After the authorities sent a police spy to the congress, the delegates moved to a boat on South Lake near Jiaxing, in Zhejiang, to escape detection. Although Soviet and Comintern delegates attended, the first congress ignored Lenin's advice to accept a temporary alliance between the Communists and the "bourgeois democrats" who also advocated national revolution; instead, they stuck to the orthodox Marxist belief that only the urban proletariat could lead a socialist revolution.

Mao was now party secretary for Hunan stationed in Changsha, and to build the party there he followed a variety of tactics. In August 1921, he founded the Self-Study University, through which readers could gain access to revolutionary literature, housed in the premises of the Society for the Study of Wang Fuzhi, a Qing dynasty Hunanese philosopher who had resisted the Manchus. He joined the YMCA Mass Education Movement to fight illiteracy, though he edited the textbooks to include radical sentiments. He continued organizing workers to strike against the administration of Hunan Governor Zhao Hengti. Yet labor issues remained central. The successful and famous Anyuan coal mines strikes (contrary to later Party historians) depended on both "proletarian" and "bourgeois" strategies. Liu Shaoqi and Li Lisan and Mao not only mobilized the miners, but formed schools and cooperatives and engaged local intellectuals, gentry, military officers, merchants, Red Gang dragon heads and even church clergy.

Mao claimed that he missed the July 1922 Second Congress of the Communist Party in Shanghai because he lost the address. Adopting Lenin's advice, the delegates agreed to an alliance with the "bourgeois democrats" of the KMT for the good of the "national revolution". Communist Party members joined the KMT, hoping to push its politics leftward. Mao enthusiastically agreed with this decision, arguing for an alliance across China's socio-economic classes. Mao was a vocal anti-imperialist and in his writings he lambasted the governments of Japan, the UK and US, describing the latter as "the most murderous of hangmen".

Now Your Ready…

The next time your cat asks about Mao Zedong, you're ready!

In my professional opinion, every time your cat asks about Mao, you read the section above **in it's entirety** until he or she stops.

This will…

- Set their mind at ease.
- Let them know how educated you are in Maos history.
- Create a launching point for you to connect with your cat on a deeper level.
- Let them know, that you know, that they know, that you know what they know, and you know.

Signs Your Cat Went Communist!

Don't be fooled

If your feline friend is a dirty commie, this book is exactly what you need, *and just in time!*

Unlike some other people, you have taken the vital first steps to free your home from communist rule. Most importantly you need to determine if your cat follows the law of the red menace or are you just a nut? Let's be honest, you shouldn't approach your cat without some solid evidence.

If this list below reveals any signs that your cat has fallen to communist rule, then and only then, you need to act fast.

Such as...

Sleeping a lot

You might not realize it but, a lazy cat is a sure-fire sign that your friend is a communist dictator. As an average hard-working citizen of society, you know the struggles of what life can bring but, when your cat starts a daily regime of naps and sleeping, it should be clear that they let go of all values. They see you as their lower-class servant and that's unacceptable. Excessive sleep is a power move that your cat doesn't respect your house and you might have noticed by now. They do little to help around the house. Once you start some basic tasks around your place, he might say something like "I'm taking a nap Chuck." and wanders off to a warm spot for some nappy time. This is a dire warning and shouldn't be taken lightly.

Oh? What do we have here?

Solution

Don't get too worked up over your sweet sleepy little commie lover. Just remember that your cat is likely doing this just to get on your nerves. That's what they want, and you can't let it get to you! I would recommend some meditation or hard liquor to calm your nerves before having "the talk."

Once you are calm and in a good mindset, make some shrimp or turkey ramen noodles for you both to enjoy and you should be able to engage the conversation tactfully and be on point. Once you rouse your cat from sleep, mention your concerns. Offer some delicious ramen noodles and hash it out properly. There is no wrong answer when it comes to a good bowl of ramen noodles as they are hard to resist, as money has been tight.

Another popular yet less successful method of approach is writing a list of chores and leaving it tucked carefully under your cats cute little sleeping paw. Most cats have not taken well to this approach and when you return after dropping off the list you might find that your cat (in the ultimate form of disrespect) has left and the list you worked on just laying on the floor or where he was napping. I never said this would be easy.

Can I has Ramen nooble? Sure buddy.

Disappearing for extended periods of time.

Don't get me started on this one! After years of extended research, scientists have found countless cats have been attending communist rallies and meetings during the evenings and nights. This might seem like an innocent outing, but these could easily build up to something more serious. The meetings lead to rallies and that leads to picketing. Once your cat gets to this point, it will be hard to get them back. They will be in the dark depths of the political party of communism and in the most extreme cases you might not get them back no matter how hard you try.

A gang of protesting cats need to be approached with extreme caution.

Even if you built up years of friendship and feel like you and your cat are top shelf pals. It might not be enough after the cold hard communist party has taken hold and filled their heads with wild propaganda and promises of free tuna and catnip. But these are the most extreme cases. For the most part, your cat is likely reading up on the history and merely testing the waters.

It doesn't happen overnight!

The simple night out with friends is usually the most innocent thing your cat can do…. If they are the right friends. Perhaps he started calling you Chuck or ignores you when you call his name? Maybe when you sit to talk to your cat, they just walk away. Maybe he got a sweet new sweater vest and refuses to tell you where he got it from? These are all classic signs that he fell down the communist hole and he is desperately calling for help.

Solution

The answer here lies in several angles. First and foremost, you need to be sure of what your cat is heading out to do during outside time. You could hire A Private Investigator to follow your kitty around for solid proof if your chubby little furball is just hanging with the boys or practicing the dark arts of communism. I personally would recommend buying a guile suit off Amazon or your favorite nutjob survival store and follow your feisty friend around town all night.

You could also get a G.P.S. (Global Positioning System) and hide in on your cat during one of your mutual agreed petting sessions. That way you can use some of this new-fangled technology to track your cat and see what stops he makes while out at night. Does he make a quick stop in Russia or China? Or is he innocently playing with smoke bombs down at the local river? You will have a detailed account of every move your cat made.

I don't think this is an old G.P.S. (But you get the idea)

Once you know what your cats motives are you can address the situation. If you find your cat is attending regular communist meetings, then I recommend changing the lock on all your doors. Once you do that, he can no longer get out and can only sit on the windowsill and watch those crunchy little birds sing in the trees.

Stuck inside.

Your cat calls you Chuck all the time.

This one is a little harder to explain but, I'll do my best. Does your cat call you chuck as a nickname? So, let's address the elephant in the room on this topic. Cats "can't" talk. Right. We know this as cat owners. We also know what our cat's are saying too. When your cat asks for food, you know. When your kitty wants outside, you know. You know what your cat is saying. It's talking to you in your special language with your tight bond you built through the years.

How disrespectful

So when you notice your sweet kitty strutting around saying things such as "Feed me, Chuck." or "Hey Chuck, lemmie outside How bout dat." Or "Chucko, you going to give some yo noms or wat?" or "It'd sure be cool if there were a lot less turds in my litter box. CHUCK!" These would be a lot less offensive if your cat didn't say Chuck all the darn time. So how do we handle this delicate situation?

Solution

Now, this all sounds extremely frightening! Your best friend would rather lick his own bunghole in a crowded room than look you in the eye. However, this could be the very point of recovery you both need as you can heal your viewpoints. Let's make this perfectly clear, the term Chuck is a communist slang word widely used amongst the party as a way to let you know that you are beneath them by a high level. As such you must fight furball with furball. If your cat refers to you as "Chuck" simply fire back and call him Larry. Doing so lets him know that you are making a connection to one of the worst movies ever made and your cat will stop in short order. Your cat knows that Kevin James is a pretty funny guy generally, but his bad movie choices hurt his career and will start to sympathize with Kevin James. Overall, that is the simplest way to stop your cat in his tracks.

Now, lets not get too cocky here. Even though most cats have heard of James, not all of them have. I know it's hard to believe but it's a simple fact. You might have to be more tactful if this is the case and more desperate measures will be needed. Normally I don't support bribery in these matters but in such an extreme case it may be the only method to handle the situation. The local market is full of tasty treats that your cat will love! I have found that most breeds of cats prefer a hefty T-Bone steak or prime rib that was seared to perfection. In a pinch you can get porkchops or even chicken but remember that these options are a far second and you shouldn't put a price on your friend like that.

Your cat doesn't pay for anything or help around the house.

Wow, this ones on you. You seriously do everything while you cat fell asleep while watching Friends reruns on the couch? I bet when your cat gets hungry you jump right up and get him or her some food too! You do? Wooooow, I cant even…

Freeloader

I guess you know where I'm going with this. Yeah, this is probably the biggest sign of all. Your cat is a communist and is darn proud of it. You get paid to only distribute your hard-earned money to your little sweet-meat roommate. Is this fair? Most certainly not and must be stopped! If your freeloading feline has taken all the benefits and contributes nothing while you slave away daily without question. I'm sorry to say, you fell right into his trap.

Solution

This time it's way too late for talking out your differences. You'll have to take this to the next level immediately. First and foremost, STOP DOING HIS LAUNDRY! Once your cat realizes that they have no clean clothes to wear, you'll have them right on the ropes! Sweater Vests are both trendy and fashionable. There is no wonder that cats hold these iconic tops to the highest regard! If he goes to get dressed in the morning and all the sweater vests are dirty, your cat will have no choice but to come to you for answers. He will understand pretty quickly where you stand in the matter and will have no choice but to wash his own clothes. CONGRADULATIONS, you just made a big step in squashing your cats lazy ways.

However, some people find it quite hard to watch their cat walk around in the nude, you should stay strong. Perhaps toss out some playful banter to help get your message across.

Such as…

"Whoa, NUDE ALERT!"

"Come on, nobody asked to see that."

"Where's that dandy new sweater vest you got for Christmas?"

The list goes on but, you get the idea. He knows you're being a jerk but, it's for the greater good.

Your cat brings you dead animals.

This can sound pretty dire but don't worry. Your cat actually brings you dead animals because of instinct and wants to share it's fresh kill with a friend (and luckily that's you… this time.) It's a fairly innocent gesture and shouldn't be cause for any alarm. Most mice are most likely government spies and most small birds are Libertarians, so no harm there really. Just remember, once your cat has gone to the extent and brought a fresh kill into your home, your next choice is very important.

Solution

Eat it. Let's not be rude here and ruin all the work that we have accomplished this far. Don't get all stuck up. People have been eating crazy stuff for eons. As a matter of fact, you have an option here. Why not make it a special night with your kitty and fry that "bad boy" up with some garlic and butter and you two can eat like kings. If you do this with a smile on your face, I'm pretty sure you and your cat could bond to the point of no return.

Once you do this one simple thing, the door is wide open to your cats' little heart, all you have to do is, step right in.

Conclusion

No matter what, remember that not all cats are evil, just most of them. Sometimes when you get home after a long day at work, you might find your cat has already fired up Mario 3 and set out a cold beer. He even would play as Luigi even though Luigi kinda sucks. That right there is a true friend, and you should by soft can food pretty consistently for that special little furball. On the other hand, you bought this book for a reason. The simple fact that communism in cats is a real threat and now you have the tools for a free house and home. Once you deal with the problem, I'd love to hear your results but there is no way I'm giving you my phone number and I don't know you well enough to give you my email. However, I am happy to report that recent tests have shown this book to have a solid 54.9% success rate and that's better than zero. So get out there and save your cat from an uncertain future.

Made in the USA
Columbia, SC
05 July 2025

60377075R00017